AA Essential

French

for kids

About this book

Jane Wightwick
had the idea

Wina Gunn
wrote the pages

Leila Gaafar (aged 10)
drew the first pictures in
each chapter

Robert Bowers
(not aged 10) drew the
other pictures, and
designed the book

Important things that **must** be included

Marie-Claude Dunleavy
did the French stuff

Distributed in the United Kingdom by
AA Publishing, Norfolk House, Priestley Road, Basingstoke,
Hampshire RG24 9NY

© **g-and-w** PUBLISHING 2000
Reprinted November 2000

A CIP catalogue record for this book is available from the
British Library

ISBN: 0 7495 2435 9

Published by **AA Publishing** (a trading name of Automobile
Association Developments Limited, whose registered office is
Norfolk House, Priestley Road, Basingstoke, Hampshire RG24
9NY. Registered number 1878835)

Printed and bound by **G. Canale & C.S.P.A.**, Torino, Italy

Cover design by **Joshua Smith Graphics**

What's inside

Making friends

How to be cool with the gang

Wanna play?

Our guide to joining in everything from hide-and-seek to the latest electronic game

Feeling hungry

Order your favourite junk or go local

Looking good

Make sure you keep up with all those essential fashions

Hanging out

At the pool, beach or theme park – don't miss out on the action

Pocket money

Spend it here!

Grown-up talk

blah! blah! blah! blah!

If you really, really have to!

Extra bits

All the handy stuff – numbers, months, time, days of the week

MAKING FRIENDS

me
moi 👄 mwa

my snake
mon serpent
👄 mo sir-pc

my friend
mon copain
👄 mo ko-pa

my dog
mon chien
👄 mo shee-a

my friend
ma copine
👄 ma ko-pe

6

my big brother
mon grand frère
🔊 mo gro frair

grandpa
papi
🔊 pah-pee

grandma
mamie
🔊 ma-mee

dad
apa
🔊 pah-pah

mum
maman
🔊 ma-mon

my little sister
ma petite sœur
🔊 ma pteet sir

MAKING FRIENDS

Half a step this way

stepfather/stepmother
beau-père/belle-mère
🔊 bow pair/bel mair

stepbrother/
stepsister
beau-frère/
belle-sœur
🔊 bow frair/bel sir

half-brother/half-sister
demi-frère/demi-sœur
🔊 demee frair/demee sir

Hi!
Salut!
👄 saloo

What's your name?
Comment tu t'appelles?
👄 ko-mo too tapel

My name's ...
Je m'appelle ...
👄 juh mapel

Are you OK?
Ça va?
👄 sa va

Cool, and you?
Ça boom, et toi?
👄 sa boom, eh twa

Kissing is extremely popular among French children. You can't possibly say hello to your friends in the morning without kissing them on both cheeks. Try this in front of your mirror if your friends in England won't let you experiment on them.

8

9

How old are you?
T'as quel âge?
👄 ta kel arj

12 years old
Douze ans
👄 dooz on

Happy birthday!
Bon anniversaire!
👄 bon anee-versair

What's your star sign?
C'est quoi, ton signe astrologique?
👄 say kwa toh seen-yastrolojeek

When's your birthday?
C'est quand, ton anniversaire
👄 say kon, ton anee-versa

French children often sing "Happy Birthday" in English when the candles are blown out on the cake. So you can practise singing the words with a French accent!

appee birzday too yo
appee birzday too yo

Star Signs

AQUARIUS
Jan. 21 – Feb. 19
le Verseau ➤ luh ver-so

PISCES
Feb. 20 – Mar. 20
les Poissons ➤ lay pwason

ARIES
Mar. 21 – Apr. 20
le Bélier ➤ luh belly-uh

TAURUS
Apr. 21 – May 21
le Taureau ➤ luh tor-oh

GEMINI
May 22 – June 21
les Gémeaux ➤ lay jem-oh

CANCER
June 22 – July 23
le Cancer ➤ luh cancer

LEO
July 24 – Aug. 23
le Lion ➤ luh lee-on

VIRGO
Aug. 24 – Sep. 23
la Vierge ➤ la vee-erj

LIBRA
Sep. 24 – Oct. 23
la Balance ➤ la ba-lons

SCORPIO
Oct. 24 – Nov. 22
le Scorpion ➤ luh scorpion

SAGITTARIUS
Nov. 23 – Dec. 21
le Sagittaire ➤ luh sajitair

CAPRICORN
Dec. 22 – Jan. 20
le Capricorne ➤ luh capricorn

11

12

football
le foot
🔊 luh foot

rollerskating/
rollerblading
le roller
🔊 luh roller

music
la musique
🔊 la mew-zeek

electronic games
les jeux électroniques
🔊 lay juh ay-lek-tro-neek

tv
la télé
🔊 la taylay

comics
la BD
🔊 la bay-day

teddies
les nounours
🔊 lay noonoor

school
l'école
🔊 lay-kol

spiders
les araignées
🔊 layz aran-nyay

13

What's your favourite ...?
Quel est ton/ta ... préféré(e)?
👄 kel ay toh/tah ... preh-fairay

group
(ton) groupe
👄 (toh) groop

colour
(ta) couleur
👄 (tah) koo-lur

→ Page 51

food
(ton) plat
👄 (toh) pla

team
(ton) équipe
👄 (toh) ekeep

animal
(ton) animal
👄 (toh) a-nee-mal

dog
le chien
👄 luh shee-an

cat
le chat
👄 luh sha

snake
le serpent
👄 luh sir-pon

guinea-pig
le corbaye
👄 luh kor-bay

hamster
le hamster
👄 luh amster

budgie
la perruche
👄 la peroosh

My little doggy goes *oua-oua-oua!*

A French doggy (that's "toutou" in baby language) doesn't say "woof, woof", it says *"oua, oua"* (*waa-waa*). A French sheep says *"bêê, bêê!"* (*bear-bear*) and a cluck-cluck in French chicken-speak is *"cot-cot"* (*ko-ko*). But a cat does say *"miaow"* and a cow *"moo"* whether they're speaking French or English!

15

science
les sciences
👄 lay see-yons

history
l'histoire
👄 lis-twar

Way unfair!

French children hardly ever have to wear uniform to school and have very long holidays: 9 weeks in the summer and another 6–7 weeks throughout the rest of the year. But before you turn green with envy, you might not like the mounds of **"devoirs de vacances"** (*duh-vwa duh vacans*), that's "vacation homework"! And if you fail your exams, the teachers could make you repeat the whole year with your little sister!

You won't make many friends saying this!

Bog off!
Dégage
👄 Day-gaj

Shut up!
La ferme!
👄 la ferm

If you're fed up with someone, and you want to say something like "you silly …!" or "you stupid …!", you can start with **"espèce de"** (which actually means "piece of …") and add anything you like. What about …

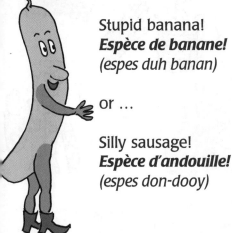

Stupid banana!
Espèce de banane!
(espes duh banan)

or …

Silly sausage!
Espèce d'andouille!
(espes don-dooy)

Take your pick. It should do the trick. You could also try **"espèce d'idiot!"** *(espes dee-dyo)*. You don't need a translation here, do you?

You might have to say

Bother!
La vache!
👄 la vash

Rats!
Zut!
👄 zoot

"Did someone call me?"

← la vache

I'm fed up
J'en ai ras le bol
👄 jon nay ral-bo

That's enough!
Y'en a marre!
👄 yona mar

I don't care
Je m'en fiche
👄 juh mon feesh

Stop it!
Arrête!
👄 aret

At last!
C'est pas trop tôt!
👄 say pah tro toe

Saying goodbye

What's your address?
Tu m'donnes ton adresse?
👄 too mdon ton adres

Here's my address
Voilà mon adresse
👄 vla mon adres

Come to visit me
Viens chez moi
👄 vya shay mwa

Write to me soon
Écris-moi vite
👄 ekree mwa veet

Have a good trip!
Bon voyage!
👄 bon vwoy-arj

Bye!
Au revoir!
👄 oh rev-wa

Bone up on your French!
How do you say goodbye
to a skeleton?

Bone Voyage!

21

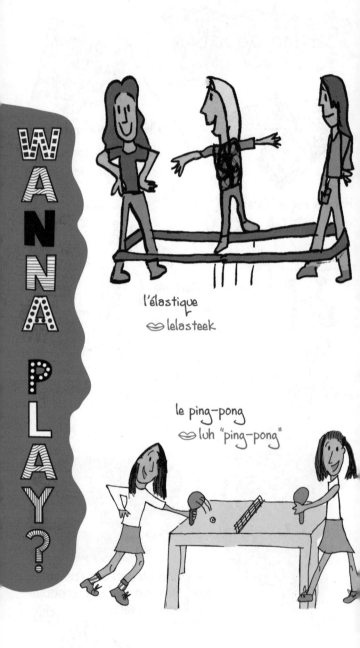

WANNA PLAY?

l'élastique
👄 lelasteek

le ping-pong
👄 luh "ping-pong"

22

la marelle
👄 la marel

le Gameboy®
👄 luh "gameboy"

les billes
👄 les bee-yuh

le yo-yo
👄 luh "yo yo"

WANNA PLAY?

23

Not now.
Pas maintenant
👄 pah mat–non

Yeah!
Ouais!
👄 oo–way

Fancy a game of **cat** or **leap sheep**?!

In France, playing tag is called playing "at cat" – *à chat* (asha). Whoever is "it" is the cat – *le chat* (luh sha). And you don't play "leap frog", you play "leap sheep" – *saute mouton* (sote moo-ton). Have you ever seen a sheep leaping? I ask you!

Electronic games

l'écran
👄 lay-kra

le modem
👄 luh "modem"

le Cédé-Rom
👄 luh say-day-rom

HIGH SCORES
Frank
Robert
Leila
Sarah
Jean-Paul
Denis
Wina
Jane

le joystick
👄 luh "joystick"

le clavier
👄 luh clavee-ay

la souris
👄 la soo-ree

28

What do I do?
Qu'est-ce que je fais?
👄 kesker juh fay

Show me
Montre-moi
👄 montruh mwa

Am I dead?
Ch'suis mort?
👄 shwee more

Shoot-em-up!
Tue-les!
👄 Tew lay

How many lives do I have?
J'ai combien de vies?
👄 jay konbee-yah duh vee

How many levels are there?
Y'a combien de niveaux?
👄 yah konbee-yah de neevo

Non couch-potato activities.

tennis
le tennis
👄 luh "tennis"

trampolining
le trampoline
👄 luh "trampoline"

bowling
le bowling
👄 luh "bowling"

swimming
la natation
👄 la natasee-on

GYM?

hockey
le hockey
👄 luh okee

gymnastics
la gymnastique
👄 la gymnasteek

ballet
le ballet
👄 luh ballay

basketball le basket
👄 luh basket

and, of course, we haven't forgotten *"le foot"* … (P.T.O.)

31

footy

boots
les godasses
🗣 lay godas

shin-pads
les protèges
🗣 lay protej

ref
l'arbitre
🗣 lar-beetruh

football kit
les affaires de foot
🗣 layz afayr duh fo

Well played!
Bien joué
🗣 beeyah joo-way

crossbar
la barre
🗣 la bar

goalpost
le poteau
🗣 luh potto

goal
le but
🗣 luh boo

goalie
le gardien
🗣 luh gardyen

Pass!
Passe!
🗣 pas

Off side!
Hors-jeu!
or-juh

You're in my team
T'es dans mon équipe
tay don mon ay-keep

Hands!
J'a eu mains!
Ya ew man

Foul!
Coup-franc!
koo fron

Penalty!
Le penalty!
luh paynalty

He pushed me!
Il m'a poussé!
eel ma poo-say

Goal!
Goal!
just say it!

33

Keeping the others in line

Not like that!
Pas comme ça!
👄 pah kom sa

You cheat!
Tricheur! (boys only)/
Tricheuse! (girls only)
👄 tree-sher/
tree-sherz

I'm not playing anymore
Je joue plus
👄 juh joo ploo

It's not fair!
C'est pas juste!
👄 say pah joos

Stop it!
Arrête!
👄 aret

Showing off

a handstand?
le poirier?
👄 luh pwa-riyay

Can you do ...
Tu sais faire ...
👄 too say fair

Look at me!
Regarde-moi!
👄 re-gard mwa

a cartwheel?
la roue?
👄 la roo

this?
ça?
👄 sa

Impress your French friends with this!

You can show off to your new French friends by practising this tongue twister:

Si ces six sausissons-ci sont six sous, ces six sausissons-ci sont très chers

see say see soseeson see son see soo, say see soseeson see son tray shair

(This means "If these six sausages cost six sous, these six sausages are very expensive.")

Then see if they can do as well with this English one:

"She sells sea shells on the sea shore, but the shells she sells aren't sea shells, I'm sure."

For a rainy day

pack of cards
un jeu de cartes
👄 uh juh duh kart

my deal/your deal
à moi la donne/à toi la donne
👄 a mwa la don/a twa la d

king
le roi
👄 luh rwa

queen
la dame
👄 la dam

jack
le valet
👄 luh valay

joker
le joker
👄 luh joka

trèfle
👄 tray-fluh

cœur
👄 kur

pique
👄 peek

carreau
👄 karo

beefburger
le steak haché
👄 luh stek ashay

chips
les frites
👄 lay freet

ice-cream
la glace
👄 la gla[s]

coke
le coca
👄 luh koka

F E E L I N G H U N G R Y

snails
les escargots
🗣 layz eskargo

mussels
les moules
🗣 lay mool

la crème caramel
🗣 la krem karamel

orange juice
le jus d'orange
🗣 luh joo doronj

FEELING HUNGRY

39

Grub (la bouffe)

I'm starving
J'ai une faim de loup
🗣 jay oon fam duh loo

That means "I have the hunger of a wolf!"

le loup

Please can I have ...
Donnez-moi, s'il vous plaît ...
🗣 donay mwa,
seel voo play

... a chocolate bun
un pain au chocolat
🗣 uh pan oh shokolah

... a croissant
un croissant
🗣 uh kruh-son

... an apple turnover
un chausson aux pommes
🗣 uh show-son oh pom

... a chocolate eclair
un éclair au chocolat
👄 un eklair oh shokolah

... a bun with raisins
un pain aux raisins
👄 uh pan oh rayzan

... a French stick
une baguette
👄 oon baget

... a pancake
une crêpe
👄 oon krep

... a waffle
une gaufre
👄 oon go-fruh

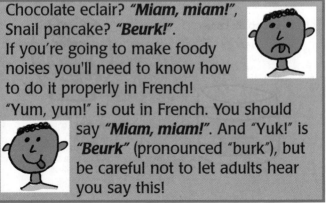

Chocolate eclair? **"Miam, miam!"**,
Snail pancake? **"Beurk!"**.
If you're going to make foody
noises you'll need to know how
to do it properly in French!
"Yum, yum!" is out in French. You should
say **"Miam, miam!"**. And "Yuk!" is
"Beurk" (pronounced "burk"), but
be careful not to let adults hear
you say this!

Drink up

I'm dying for a drink
Je meurs de soif
👄 juh mur duh swaf

I'd like ...
Je voudrais ...
👄 juh voodray

... a coke
... un coca
👄 uh koka

... an orange juice
... un jus d'orange
👄 uh joo doronj

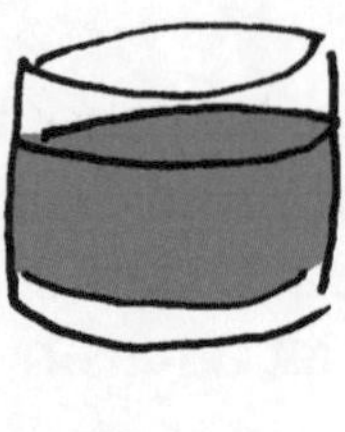

... an apple juice
... un jus de pommes
👄 uh joo duh pom

You can also have your lemonade with squash – then it's called a "***diablo***". The most well-known is "***diablo de menthe***", lemonade with mint squash – hmmm!

... a lemonade
... une limonade
🕪 oon leemonad

... a squash
un sirop
🕪 uh seero

... a milkshake
... un milkshake
🕪 uh meelkshek

You get your hot chocolate in a bowl (and that, at least, is a decent amount).

... a hot chocolate
... un chocolat
🕪 uh shokolah

Did you know?

A lot of children have hot chocolate for breakfast in the morning and some of them will dip their croissants or bread in it. It goes all soggy and Mum is sure not to like this!

How did you like it?

That's lovely
C'est super-bon
👄 say soopair-bon

That's gorgeous
C'est géant
👄 say jay-on

I don't like that
J'aime pas ça
👄 jem pah sa

I'm stuffed
J'ai trop bouffé
👄 jay troh boofay

I can't eat that
Je mange pas ça
👄 juh monj pah sa

That's gross
C'est dégoutant
👄 say day-gooton

A "crunchy man" sandwich, please.

You never thought you could crunch up a man in France and get away with it, did you? Well, in France a cheese-and-ham toastie is:

un croque-monsieur

👄 uh krok murs-yur

… that means a "crunchy man". There's also a "crunchy woman".

un croque-madame

👄 uh krok ma-dam

… which is the same but with a fried egg on top.

Tales of snails

Did you know that snails have to be put in a bucket of salt water for three days to clean out their insides (don't ask!). After that they are baked in the oven in their shells and eaten with loads of garlic butter. And many French kids still love them!

LOOKING GOOD

nail varnish
le vernis à ongles
👄 luh ver-nee a ong-luh

headband
le bandeau
👄 luh band-c

bracelets
les bracelets
👄 lay bracelay

braid
la natte
👄 la na

crop top
le débardeur
👄 luh debad

belt
la ceinture
👄 la santee-your

miniskirt
la minijupe
👄 la minee-joop

shoes
les chaussures
👄 lay show-sur

bike
le vélo
👄 luh vaylo

46

cap
la casquette
👄 la kasket

le T-shirt
👄 luh "T-shirt"

tattoo
le tatouage
👄 luh tattoo-arj

le jean
👄 luh jeen

le walkman
👄 luh "walkman"

le skate-board
👄 luh "skateboard"

trainers
les baskets
👄 lay basket

LOOKING GOOD

47

That T-shirt, please
Ce T-shirt-là, s'il vous plaît
🗣 suh "T-shirt" la, seel voo play

Cool tattoo!
Tatouage cool!!
🗣 tattoo-arj cool

The pink frilly one
Le rose à frous-frous
🗣 luh roz a froo froo

A braid, please
Une natte, s'il vous plaît
🗣 oon nat, seel voo play

The purple stripey one
Le violet à rayure
🗣 luh vee-oh-la a rayure

Awesome miniskirt!
Minijupe d'enfer!
🗣 minee-joop donfair

Where's my skateboard?
Où est mon skate-board?
🗣 oo ay mon "skateboard"

Sounds alike, but ...

Watch out for French words that sound like English but mean something different. For example, **"une veste"** in French is "a jacket" and not something you wear with your knickers!

spotty
à pois
👄 a pwa

flowery
à fleurs
👄 a flur

frilly
à frous-frous
👄 a froo froo

glittery
à paillettes
👄 a pie-et

stripey
à rayures
👄 a rayure

49

jeans
le jean
👄 luh "jean"

T-shirt
le T-shirt
👄 luh "T-shirt"

sweatshirt
le sweat
👄 luh swet

trainers
les baskets
👄 lay basket

dress
la robe
👄 la rob

skirt
la jupe
👄 la joop

trousers
le pantalon
👄 luh panta...

football strip
le maillot de foot
👄 luh mayo duh foot

shorts
le short
👄 luh "short"

shoes
les chaussures
👄 lay show-soor

50

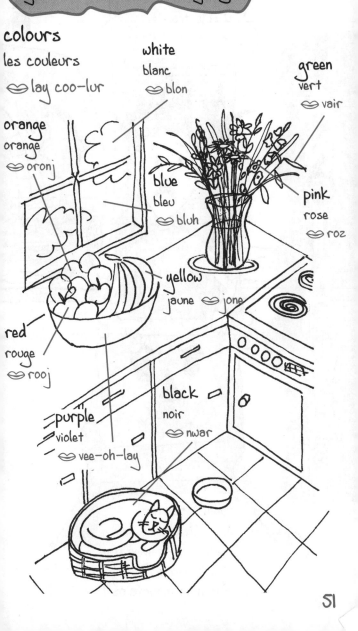

Colour this page yourself
(you can't expect us to do everything!)

colours
les couleurs
— lay coo-lur

white
blanc
— blon

green
vert
— vair

orange
orange
— oronj

blue
bleu
— bluh

pink
rose
— roz

yellow
jaune — jone

red
rouge
— rooj

black
noir
— nwar

purple
violet
— vee-oh-lay

51

What shall we do?
Qu'est-ce qu'on fait?
🗨 kesk on fay

Can I come?
Je peux venir?
🗨 juh puh vuneer

Where do you lot hang out?
Où trainez-vous?
🗨 oo trainay voo

That's really wicked
C'est géant
🗨 say jay-on

I'm (not) allowed
J'ai (pas) le droit
🗨 jay (pa) luh drwa

Beach babies

Can I borrow this?
Tu me prêtes ça?
🔊 too muh pret sa

Let's hit the beac...
On va à la plage
🔊 on va a la plarj

Is this your bucket?
C'est ton seau?
🔊 say toh so

You can bury me
Tu peux m'enterrer
🔊 too puh moterray

Stop throwing sand!
Arrête de jeter du sable!
🔊 arret duh jetay dew sabluh

Mind my eyes!
Attention à mes yeux!
🔊 attensee–on
a maiz yuh

sea
la mer
🗣 la mair

beach
la plage
🗣 la plarj

sandcastle
le château de sable
🗣 luh shato duh sabluh

towel
la serviette
🗣 la sir-vee-et

swimming costume
le maillot
🗣 luh my-yo

bucket
le seau
🗣 luh so

spade
la pelle
🗣 la pel

snorkel
le tuba
🗣 luh tew-ba

shells
les coquillages
🗣 lay kokeeyarj

How to get rid of your parents and eat lots of chocolate!

In France there are great beach clubs that organize all sorts of games as well as competitions (sandcastles, sports, etc.). The prizes are often given by large companies who make kids' stuff such as chocolate and toys. Insist on signing up!

It's going swimmingly!

How to make a splash in French

PLOUF

Let's hit the swimming pool
On va à la piscine
👄 on va a la piseen

Can you swim (underwater)?
Tu sais nager (sous l'eau)?
👄 too say najay (soo lo)

Me too/
I can't
Moi aussi/Moi pas
👄 mwa os-see/
mwa pa

I'm getting changed
Je me change
👄 juh muh shanj

Can you dive?
Tu sais plonger?
👄 too say plonjay

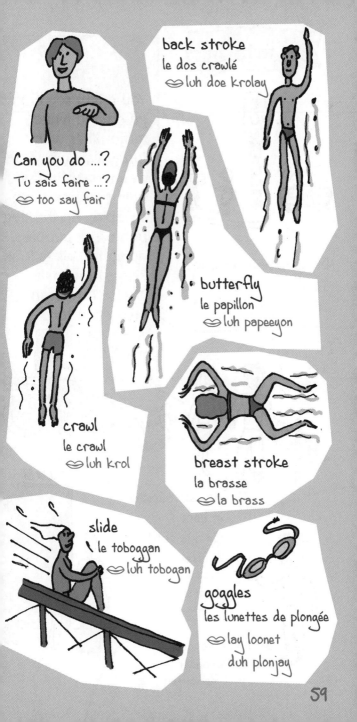

back stroke
le dos crawlé
👄 luh doe krolay

Can you do ...?
Tu sais faire ...?
👄 too say fair

butterfly
le papillon
👄 luh papeeyon

crawl
le crawl
👄 luh krol

breast stroke
la brasse
👄 la brass

slide
le toboggan
👄 luh tobogan

goggles
les lunettes de plongée
👄 lay loonet
duh plonjay

Downtown

Pooper-scoopers on wheels!

You might see bright green-and-white motorbikes with funny vacuum cleaners on the side riding around town scooping up the dog poop. The people riding the bikes look like astronauts! (Well, you'd want protection too, wouldn't you?)

Do you know the way?
Tu connais le chemin?
☞ too konay luh shema

Is it far?
C'est loin?
☞ say lwan

Are we allowed in here?
On a le droit d'entrer ici?
☞ on a luh drwa dentray eessee

Let's ask
On va démander
☞ o va demonday

60

playground
l'aire de jeu
⊜ lair duh juh

slide
le toboggan
⊜ luh tobogan

park
le parc
⊜ luh park

swings
la balançoire
⊜ la balonswar

...us
...e bus
⊜ luh boos

car
la bagnole
⊜ la banyol

The "proper" French word for car is *"voiture"* (*vwat-yure*), but you'll look very uncool saying this. Stick to *"bagnole"* (*banyol*), or if the car is a wreck, try *"tacot"* (*taco*) for even more street cred: *"Quel tacot!"* (*kel tako* – "What an old banger!").

61

Picnic (le pique-nique)

I hate wasps
Je déteste les guêpes
👄 juh daytest lay gep

Move over!
Pousse-toi!
👄 poos twa

bread
le pain
👄 luh pan

Let's sit here
On s'assoie ici?
👄 on saswa ees:

napkin
la serviette
👄 la sir-vee-et

ham
le jambon
👄 luh jambon

cheese
le fromage
👄 luh fromarj

yoghurt
le yaourt
👄 luh ya-oort

crisps
les chips
👄 lay sheep

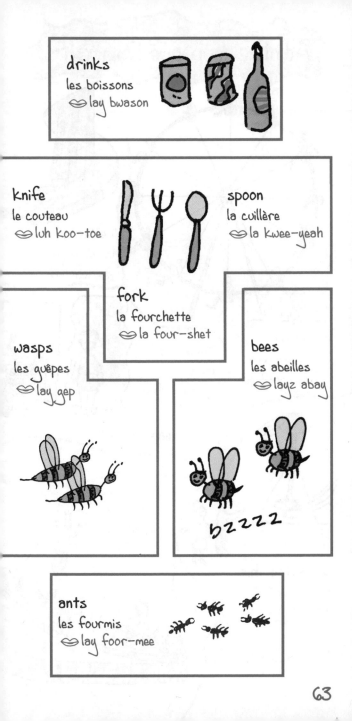

drinks
les boissons
👄 lay bwason

knife
le couteau
👄 luh koo-toe

spoon
la cuillère
👄 la kwee-yeah

fork
la fourchette
👄 la four-shet

wasps
les guêpes
👄 lay gep

bees
les abeilles
👄 layz abay

bzzzz

ants
les fourmis
👄 lay foor-mee

63

All the fun of the fair

helter-skelter
le toboggan
👄 luh tobogan

big wheel
la grande roue
👄 la grond roo

house of mirrors
le palais des glaces
👄 luh palay day glas

dodge-ems
les autos tamponneuses
👄 layz oto tomponerz

Let's try this
On essaie ça?
👄 on essay sa

roundabout
le manège
👄 luh manayj

It's (too) fast
Ca va (trop) vite
👄 sa va (tro) veet

That's for babies
C'est pour les petits
👄 say poor lay ptee

Do you get wet in here?
On sort mouillé d'ici?
👄 on sor moo-yay deessee

I'm not going on my own
J'y vais pas tout seul
👄 jee vay pa too surl

65

Spend it here

sweets
les bonbons
👄 lay bonbon

les T-shirts
👄 lay "T-shir

toys
les jouets
👄 lay joo-ay

le vendeur
👄 luh von-

POCKET MONEY

books
les livres
🗢 lay lee-vruh

le mobile
🗢 luh mobeel

les crayons
🗢 lay crayon
Watch out!
This means *pencils*
NOT crayons!

What does that sign say?

Boucherie

boucherie
butcher shop
〜 booshree

pâtisserie
cake shop
〜 pateesree

Pâtisserie

boulangerie
bakery
〜 boolonjree

Boulangerie

confiserie
sweet shop
〜 konfeesree

épicerie

papeterie
stationers
〜 paptree

PAPETERIE

épicerie
grocery sho[p]
〜 aypeesree

boutique de vêtements
clothes shop
〜 booteek duh vetmon

Boutique de vêtements

Money talk

French money is **francs** (pronounced *fron*).
1 **franc** is 100 **centimes** (*senteem*).

Coins: 5, 10, 20, 50 **centimes**

1, 2, 5, 10, 20 **francs**

Notes: 20, 50, 100, 200, 500 **francs**

Make sure you know how much you are spending
before you blow all your pocket money in one go!

68

Do you have some dosh?
T'as des sous?
👄 tah day soo

I'm skint
Je suis fauché
👄 juh swee foshay

I'm loaded
J'ai plein d'sou
👄 jay pla dsoo

Here you go
Voilà
👄 vla

Can you lend me ten francs?
Tu peux me prêter dix franc
👄 too puh muh pretay dee fron

No way!
Pas question!
👄 pa kes-tyo

That's a bargain
C'est pas cher
👄 say pa shair

It's a rip off
C'est du vol
👄 say dew vol

69

Sweet heaven!

I love this shop
J'adore cette boutique
👄 jadore set booteek

Let's get some sweets
On va acheter des bonbons
👄 on va ashtay day bonbon

Let's get an ice cream
On va acheter une glace
👄 on va ashtay oon glas

lollipops
des sucettes
👄 day sooset

a bar of chocolate
une tablette de chocolat
👄 oon tablet duh shokola

chewing gum
chewing gum
👄 just say it, will you!

If you really want to look French and end up with lots of fillings ask for:

des Carambars™
(day caram–bar)

medium-hard toffee-bars, now also available in all sorts of fruity flavours – also popular for the desperately silly jokes to be found inside the wrappings

des Malabars™ (day malabar)

bubble-gum, also popular for the tattoos provided with them

des nounours en chocolat
(day noonoor on shokola)

teddy-shaped marshmallow-type sweets in chocolate coating

des frites (day freet)

fruity gums, slightly fizzy, shaped like chips

des Mini Berlingot™ (day mini berlingo)

sugary creamy stuff sold in small squidgy packets – a bit like a small version of the "lunchbox" yoghurts

des Dragibus™ (day drajibus)

multi-coloured licorice jelly beans

... colouring pencils
des crayons de couleur
😊 day krayon duh koolur

I'm getting ...
J'achète ... 😊 jashait

... stamps
des timbres
😊 day timbruh

... felt tip pens
des feutres
😊 day fuh-truh

... a pen
un stylo
😊 uh stee-lo

... a cassette
une cassette
😊 oon "cassette"

... a CD
un CD
😊 uh say-day

... comics
des BD
😊 day bay day

For many years France's favourite comics have been Astérix and Tintin. They have both been translated into English, as well as into many other languages. Today children also like to read:

Tom Tom et Nana
Boule et Bill
Natacha
Gaston Lagaffe

73

Help!

Something has dropped/broken
Quelque chose est tombé/cassé
👄 kel-ker shose ay tombay/kassay

Please
S'il vous plaît
👄 seel voo play

Can you help me?
Vous pouvez m'aider?
👄 voo poovay mayday

Where's the letter box?
Où est la boîte aux lettres?
👄 oo ay la bwat oh lettruh

Where are the toilets?
Où sont les toilettes?
👄 oo son lay twalet

I can't manage it
Je n'y arrive pas
👄 juh nee arreev pah

Could you pass me that?
Vous pouvez me passer ça?
👄 Voo poovay muh passay sa

What's the time?
Quelle heure il est?
👄 kel ur eelay

Come and see
Venez voir
👄 venay vwar

May I look at your watch?
Je peux voir sur votre montre?
👄 jer puh vwar syur votruh montruh

Lost for words

... my ticket
mon billet
👄 mo beeyay

I've lost ...
J'ai perdu ...
👄 jay perdew

... my bike
mon vélo
👄 mo vaylo

... my parents
mes parents
👄 may paron

... my shoes
mes chaussures
👄 may sho-syur

... my money
mon argent
👄 mo arjon

... my jumper
mon pull
👄 mo pool

... my watch
ma montre
👄 ma montruh

... my jacket
ma veste
👄 ma vest

79

Show this page to adults who can't seem to make themselves clear (it happens). They will point to a phrase, you read what they mean and you should all understand each other perfectly.

Ne t'en fais pas
Don't worry

Assieds-toi ici
Sit down here

Quel est ton nom et ton prénom?
What's your name and surname?

Quel âge as-tu?
How old are you?

D'où viens-tu?
Where are you from?

Où habites-tu?
Where are you staying?

Où est-ce que tu as mal?
Where does it hurt?

Est-ce que tu es allergique à quelque chose?
Are you allergic to anything?

C'est interdit
It's forbidden

Tu dois être accompagné d'un adulte
You have to have an adult with you

Je vais chercher quelqu'un qui parle anglais
I'll get someone who speaks English

There was an English cat called "one, two, three" and a French cat called "un, deux, trois" standing waiting to cross a river. Both were afraid of water, so the English cat suggested that they race across to make it more fun. Who won?

Answer: "One, two, three" because "un, deux, trois" CAT SANK!

un   un

deux   duh

trois   twa

quatre   katruh

cinq   sank

six   👄 sees

sept   👄 set

huit   👄 weet

neuf   👄 nuf

dix   👄 dees

onze   👄 onz

douze   👄 dooz

83

13 treize	*trez*	17 dix-sept	*dees-set*
14 quatorze	*catorz*	18 dix-huit	*dees-weet*
15 quinze	*kanz*	19 dix-neuf	*dees-nuf*
16 seize	*sez*	20 vingt	*van*

If you want to say "twenty-two", "sixty-five" and so on, you can just put the two numbers together like you do in English:

22 **vingt-deux**   *van duh*

65 **soixante cinq** *swasont sank*

This works except if you're saying "twenty-one", "sixty-one" and so on. Then you need to add the word for "and" (**et**) in the middle:

21 **vingt et un**   *vant eh un*

61 **soixante et un** *swasont eh un*

30 trente	*tront*
40 quarante	*karont*
50 cinquante	*sankont*
60 soixante	*swasont*
70 soixante-dix	*swasont dees*
80 quatre-vingts	*katruh van*
90 quatre-vingt-dix	*katruh van dees*
100 cent	*sonn*

The French must be really keen on sums! Everything's fine until you reach 70. Instead of saying "seventy", they say "sixty-ten" (*soixante-dix*) and keep counting like this until they reach 80. So 72 is "sixty-twelve" (*soixante douze*), 78 is "sixty-eighteen" (*soixante dix-huit*), and so on.

Just so it doesn't get too easy, for 80 they say "4 twenties"! And to really make your brain ache they continue counting like this until a hundred. So 90 is "4 twenties 10" (*quatre-vingt-dix*), 95 is "4 twenties fifteen" (*quatre-vingt-quinze*) … you have remembered your calculator, haven't you??

March	mars	*mars*
April	avril	*avreel*
May	mai	*meh*

June	juin	*joo-wah*
July	juillet	*joowee-eh*
August	août	*oot*

86

September	septembre	*septombruh*
October	octobre	*octobruh*
November	novembre	*novombruh*

December	décembre	*desombruh*
January	janvier	*jonvee-eh*
February	février	*fevree-eh*

printemps *prantom*

SPRING

été *eteh*

SUMMER

automne *awtom*

AUTUMN

hiver *eever*

WINTER

Monday	lundi	*lundee*
Tuesday	mardi	*mardee*
Wednesday	mercredi	*mecredee*
Thursday	jeudi	*jurdee*
Friday	vendredi	*vendredee*
Saturday	samedi	*samdee*
Sunday	dimanche	*deemonsh*

By the way, French kids are usually off school on Wednesdays, but they have to go on Saturday mornings. Still – that's half a day less than you!

Good times

It's ...
Il est ...
🗨 eel ay

(one) o'clock
(une) heure
🗨 (oon) ur

quarter past (two)
(deux heures) et quart
🗨 (duh zur) ay kar

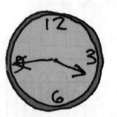

quarter to (four)
(quatre heures) moins le quart
🗨 (katr ur) mwan luh kar

half past (three)
(trois heures) et demie
🗨 (twa zur) ay demee

five past (ten)
(dix heures) cinq
👄 dees ur sank

twenty past (eleven)
(onze heures) vingt
👄 onz ur van

ten to (four)
(quatre heures) moins dix
👄 (katr ur) mwan dees

twenty to (six)
(six heures) moins vingt
👄 (sees ur) mwan van

morning
matin
🗣 ma-tah

midday
midi
🗣 meedee

afternoon
après-midi
🗣 apray meedee

midnight
minuit
🗣 meenwee

evening
soir
🗣 swar

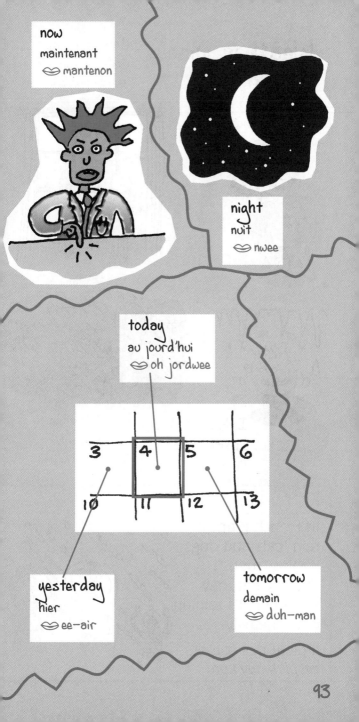

now
maintenant
👄 mantenon

night
nuit
👄 nwee

today
au jourd'hui
👄 oh jordwee

3 4 5 6
10 11 12 13

yesterday
hier
👄 ee-air

tomorrow
demain
👄 duh-man

93

Weather wise

Can we go out?
On peut sortir?
👄 on puh sorteer

It's hot
Il fait chaud
👄 eel fay show

It's cold
Il fait froid
👄 eel fay frwa

It's horrible
Il fait mauvais
👄 eel fay movay

It's raining ropes!

In French it doesn't rain "cats and dogs", it rains "ropes"! That's what they say when it's raining really heavily:

Il pleut des cordes
eel pluh day kord

95